HOW-TO LIBRARY

CRAFTING WITH DUCT TAPE

By Dana Meachen Rau • Illustrated by Kathleen Petelinsek

CHERRY LAKE PUBLISHING • ANN ARBOR, MICHIGAN

CHERRY LAKE
Publishing

Published in the United States of America by Cherry Lake Publishing
Ann Arbor, Michigan
www.cherrylakepublishing.com

Content Adviser: Dr. Julia Hovanec, Department of Arts Education and
Crafts, Kutztown University of Pennsylvania, Kutztown, Pennsylvania

Photo Credits: Page 4, ©Henrik Larsson/Shutterstock, Inc.; page
5, ©Jovani Carlo Gorospe/Dreamstime.com; page 6, ©Ian 2010/
Shutterstock, Inc.; page 7, ©iStockphoto.com/OliverChilds.

Library of Congress Cataloging-in-Publication Data
Rau, Dana Meachen, 1971–
    Crafting with duct tape / by Dana Meachen Rau.
        pages cm. — (How-to library) (Crafts)
    Audience: Grade 4 to 6.
    Includes bibliographical references and index.
    ISBN 978-1-62431-147-5 (library binding) —
ISBN 978-1-62431-279-3 (paperback) —
ISBN 978-1-62431-213-7 (e-book)
1. Tape craft—Juvenile literature. 2. Duct tape—Juvenile literature.
I. Title.
    TT869.7.R38 2013
    745.5—dc23   2013009516

Cherry Lake Publishing would like to acknowledge the work
of The Partnership for 21st Century Skills. Please visit www.p21.org
for more information.

Printed in the United States of America
Corporate Graphics Inc.
July 2013
CLFA13

A NOTE TO ADULTS:
Please review the instructions
for these craft projects before
your children make them. Be
sure to help them with any
steps you do not think they can
safely do on their own.

A NOTE TO KIDS:
Be sure to ask an adult
for help with these
craft activities when you
need it. Always put you
safety first!

HOW-TO LIBRARY

TABLE OF CONTENTS

Ideas That Stick!

Are you full of creative ideas? Creative people aren't just good at drawing or writing. Creative people are often **resourceful**, too. They can find clever solutions to problems. They invent useful objects. Sometimes they do this by using an item for a different job than it was intended.

   Duct tape was created to help people seal and fix things. But you can use it to be resourceful! Think of other ways to use duct tape. You can transform this sticky stuff into objects you can use. You can also use duct tape to decorate objects you already have.

Duct tape is a very useful tool.

Duct tape is a pressure sensitive **adhesive**. "Pressure sensitive" means very little force is needed to make it stick. When you lay duct tape on a surface, you just need to swipe it with your hand to make a strong **bond**.

Get inspired! What ideas do you have for transforming a roll of duct tape into a new creation?

Which colors will you choose for your projects?

THE THREE LAYERS OF DUCT TAPE
- The top layer is a flexible plastic coating to make the tape waterproof.
- The middle layer is cotton fabric. This makes the tape strong, flexible, and able to be cut or torn easily.
- The bottom layer is a sticky adhesive made of rubber. It can form a bond with most surfaces.

Fix-It Tape

A duck's feathers keep its body warm and dry as it swims.

During World War II (1939–1945), soldiers needed a way to keep their **ammunition** cases dry. They needed a tape that was strong and waterproof. Duct tape was the perfect solution. Soldiers found lots of uses for this tape, including fixing equipment and making bandages. They called it "duck tape" because it was waterproof, just like the feathers of a duck.

After the war, duct tape was at first mainly used by heating and cooling **technicians**, who built and repaired the ductwork in homes and buildings. They used the sticky, flexible tape to connect and patch the ducts.

Technicians eventually realized that duct tape wasn't actually good at sealing ducts. But the name stuck. People found lots of other resourceful uses for duct tape. They could patch holes in a bucket. They could hold mailboxes to posts. They could repair almost anything, indoors or out! Today, many people keep a roll of duct tape in their toolboxes or kitchen drawers. Astronauts even bring duct tape into space.

The tape used in the war was army green. The tape used by technicians was gray. Today, duct tape comes in a rainbow of colors and patterns to use for crafts. Think of ways to color your world with duct tape!

Duct tape can even be used to make a boat!

Basic Tools

You need duct tape to make all of the projects in this book! But you will also need some other tools and materials. You can find these supplies in your local craft store, superstore, or hardware store.

Duct Tape

Duct tape comes in rolls. These rolls are wrapped in plastic so that they don't stick to each other on the shelves. You can make a project with just one color of duct tape. But if you want to make stripes or other designs, buy a few rolls in different colors and patterns. Duct tape is about 2 inches (5 centimeters) wide.

Cutting Tools

Because duct tape is made of fabric, you can rip it into smaller pieces. You can rip it down the middle, too, if you want a thinner strip. But you will need scissors or a craft knife to get a clean edge.

Craft knives are extremely sharp, so always ask an adult for help when you use one. If you use a craft knife, you will also need a cutting mat.

Work Surfaces

For some projects, you will need to lay the tape sticky side down. But you don't want it to stick to your work surface. Tape peels up easily from a cutting mat. If you don't have a cutting mat, you can cover your work surface with wax paper. Tape the wax paper down with painter's tape. (Painter's tape is made to unpeel easily from surfaces.)

Yardstick, Ruler, and Flexible Tape Measure

You need tools to help you measure your duct tape. A yardstick works well for long measurements. A ruler works for shorter ones. Use a flexible tape measure when you have to measure around an object.

WAX PAPER

BE CAREFUL!
Try not to get duct tape stuck on yourself—it can hurt when you pull it off your skin.

Making Fabric Strips and Sheets

Depending on your project, you may need strips or sheets of duct tape "fabric" with tape on both sides. These strips and sheets can then be made into bags, wallets, cell phone cases, or anything else you can imagine.

Steps to make a two-sided strip

1. Cut two strips of duct tape the same length.
2. Lay one strip on your work surface, sticky side up.
3. Carefully place the center of the other piece, sticky side down, on top of the first piece. Start by just touching the centers together. Line them up the best you can. The longer the piece, the more difficult it will be to line up.
4. Drop down each side. Work slowly and carefully. Working with a partner can make this project easier. Flatten from the center to the ends with your hands, pushing out any air bubbles. You now have a two-sided strip of fabric.

Steps to make a handle

1. Cut two strips of duct tape. One of them should be about 2 inches (5 cm) shorter than the other.

2. Lay the longer strip on your work surface, sticky side up. Place the center of the shorter piece, sticky side down, on top of the first. The sticky side of the bottom strip will extend about 1 inch (2.5 cm) on each end.

3. Cut the strip in half the long way.

4. Fold the center of each strip in half the long way. Be careful not to fold the sticky ends. Now you have two handles to use for a project. Simply attach the sticky ends to any creation that needs handles!

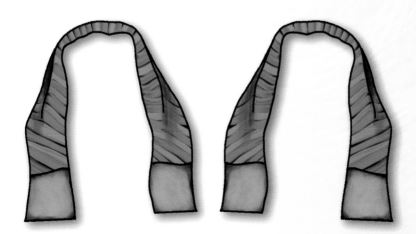

Steps to make a two-sided sheet of fabric

1. Lay a strip of duct tape sticky side up on your surface. Lay a strip sticky side down, overlapping the first about 1 inch (2.5 cm).

2. Flip your sheet of fabric over to the back. Add on another strip, slightly overlapping the one above.

3. Flip it over to the front. Lay down another strip.

4. Continue flipping from back to front, adding strips until you reach the size you want.

5. Trim the edges to neaten them. Now you have a useful sheet of duct tape fabric. You can use it to make many different crafts. What projects would you like to try?

To make striped fabric, alternate the color of duct tape strips you use.

Making Tabs

Tabs are small pieces of duct tape that are half fabric and half sticky. You can use them to make flaps, fringe, and other details for your duct tape creations.

Steps to make a square flap
1. Cut a piece of duct tape that is about 6 inches (15 cm) long.
2. Fold over about 2 inches (5 cm) of the tape from one end, and stick it to itself. Press it flat. Now part of the strip is fabric, and part is sticky.

Steps to make fringe
1. Make a square flap.
2. Use scissors to cut slots into the fabric side from the folded edge.

Steps to make a triangle flap
1. Cut a piece of duct tape that is about 3 inches (8 cm) long.
2. Fold one corner into the center. Fold the opposite corner into the center. Press flat. Now you have 1 inch (2.5 cm) of triangle fabric and 2 inches (5 cm) of sticky surface.
3. You can also make a triangle by folding the bottom edge over to a side edge. Then you'll have 2 inches (5 cm) of triangle fabric and 1 inch (2.5 cm) of sticky surface.

Fringe Flowers

Nothing brightens up someone's day like a bouquet of flowers.
Practice your duct tape tab-making skills to create a flower
that is bursting with color.

Materials

- Plastic drinking straw
- Green duct tape
- 2 other solid colors of duct tape
  (color A and color B)
- Ruler
- Scissors

Steps

1. Make six fringe tabs for each flower (*see page 13*), three with color A and three with color B.
2. Place the end of the straw on a color A tab. Roll it around the straw and press to seal.
3. Place that wrapped straw on a color B tab, lining up the fringe ends. Roll it around the straw and press to seal.

A

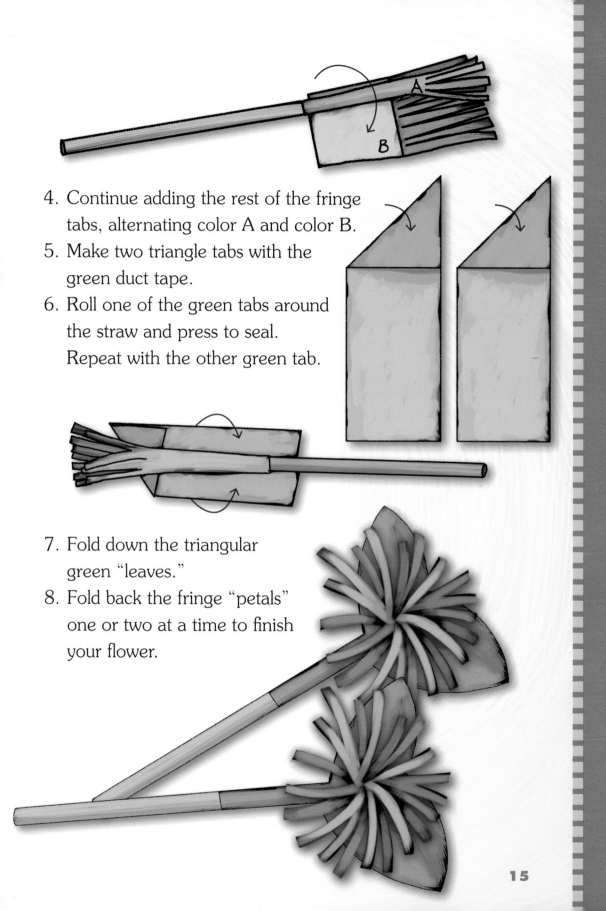

4. Continue adding the rest of the fringe tabs, alternating color A and color B.
5. Make two triangle tabs with the green duct tape.
6. Roll one of the green tabs around the straw and press to seal. Repeat with the other green tab.

7. Fold down the triangular green "leaves."
8. Fold back the fringe "petals" one or two at a time to finish your flower.

A Colorful Meal

Are you in charge of setting the table for dinner? Bring some color and creativity to the table with duct tape place mats. Turn any chore into a party!

Materials

- 3 colors/patterns of duct tape (colors A, B, and C)
- Ruler
- Scissors

Steps

1. Make five 15-inch (38 cm) two-sided strips of color A. Make six 10-inch (25 cm) two-sided strips of color B (*see page 10*).

2. Cut an 8-inch (20 cm) strip of color C. Lay it sticky side up on the work surface. Place the ends of the color A strips along the color C strip, overlapping about 1 inch (2.5 cm).

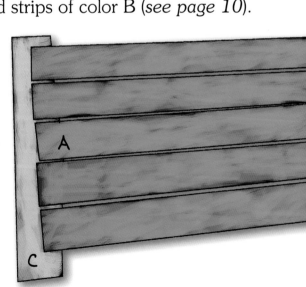

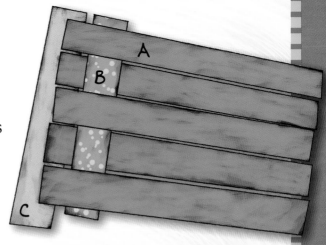

3. Weave a color B strip over and under the color A strips as shown. To weave, start by placing the color B strip beneath the first color A strip. Place it on top of the next color A strip. Alternate between placing the color B strip under and on top of the color A strips.

4. Weave a second strip of color B in the opposite way you wove the first strip. If you started under color A for the first strip, start on top of color A for this strip. Continue weaving the rest of the color B strips until you reach the end.

5. Fold over the color C strip on the end to help hold all of the strips in place. Trim the ends.

6. If needed, trim the edges on the other three sides so that all the strips are even.

7. Lay a strip of color C on the opposite edge, overlapping about 1 inch (2.5 cm). Fold over and trim the edges. Then lay strips along the top and bottom. Fold over and trim.

Jazzy Jars

Jazz up an old glass jar or drinking glass to make a vase for flowers, a pencil holder, or a container for other things. Try different combinations of colors and tabs to give your vase a unique look.

Materials
- A glass jar or drinking glass
- 2 colors/patterns of duct tape (color A and color B)
- Ruler
- Scissors

Steps
1. Make a bunch of square tabs (*see page 13*). The amount you need will depend on the size of your jar. Cut the square tabs in half to make them into rectangular tabs.

2. Starting at the bottom of the jar, stick the tabs around the jar, alternating color A and color B. The tabs should extend about ¼ inch (6 millimeters) beyond the bottom of the jar.

3. Add a second row of tabs above the first. Alternate the pattern so that color A sits above color B.

4. Add a third row, fourth row, and then as many as you need to reach the top of the jar. When you get to the last row, fold the sticky parts of the tabs over the rim of the jar.

5. Turn the jar upside down. Fold the tabs downward so they poke out. Then flip the jar right side up.

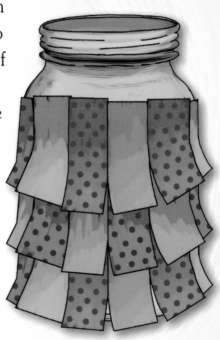

Reversible Belt

You can wear some duct tape projects! A belt adds flair to any outfit. By using two patterns of duct tape, you can wear the belt two ways. You'll have two belts in one!

Materials

- 2 patterns of duct tape
  (pattern A and pattern B)
- Scissors
- Tape measure
- Yardstick
- 2 D-ring belt fasteners (buy these at a craft or fabric store or remove them from an old belt)

Steps

1. Measure your waist with a tape measure. Then add about 6 inches (15 cm). Use this measurement to cut a strip of pattern A and pattern B.
2. Stick these strips together to make a two-sided strip (*see page 10*). Because these pieces are long, they will be hard to line up perfectly. But because you will be cutting the strip, you don't have to be too **precise**.
3. Cut the two-sided strip to fit inside the width of your belt rings.
4. Thread the end of the two-sided strip into both rings. Fold over the end about 2 inches (5 cm). Secure with a piece of duct tape.

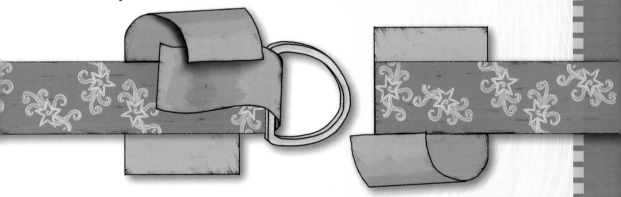

5. **Reinforce** the other end of the strip with a piece of duct tape, too.
6. To wear the belt, insert the strip through both rings. Then thread the end back through one ring. Pull to tighten.

Pencil Case

Go to school in style
with a **durable** zippered case. Use it
to hold all your pens, pencils, and other supplies.

Materials

- 8-inch (20 cm) zipper (buy this at a craft or fabric store)
- Duct tape in any color or pattern
- Ruler
- Scissors

Steps

1. Tape the ends of the zipper with small pieces of duct tape. Then place a strip of duct tape about 10 inches (25 cm) wide along one side of the zipper.
2. Flip it over.

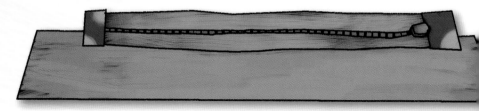

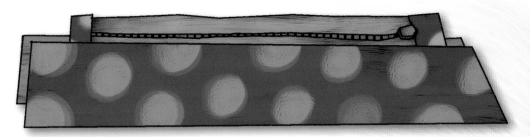

3. Lay another piece of duct tape over the first to start your fabric (*see page 12*).

4. Flip the strip over to the front. Continue making fabric until it measures about 5 inches (13 cm) long. Fold over or trim the bottom sticky edge.

5. Repeat steps 1 to 3 on the other side of the zipper.

6. Trim both side edges so they are even.

7. Fold down the sides of the case, with the zipper at the top. Tape the bottom edges closed with strips of duct tape. Trim the ends.

8. Close the two sides with strips of duct tape. Trim the ends.

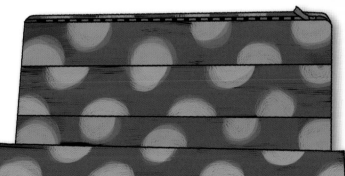

TOTE BAG

To make a tote bag, start with a longer zipper. Make your fabric wider and longer. Add two handles to the sides, near the zipper. Now you have a tote bag!

Cheer-Up Tissue Box

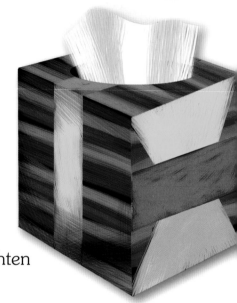

Does a runny nose and scratchy cough get you down? Decorate a box of tissues in fun, cheery colors to brighten up your next sick day.

Materials
- Tissue box
- 2 colors/patterns of duct tape (color A and color B)
- Scissors
- Craft knife

Steps
1. Unfold the box of tissues. Be careful not to rip it where it is glued. Remove the tissues and set them aside. Be careful not to pull them apart. Lay the box out flat.

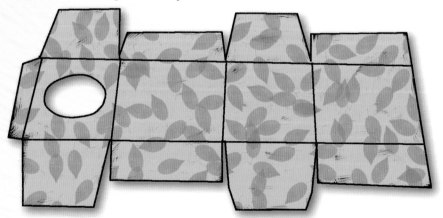

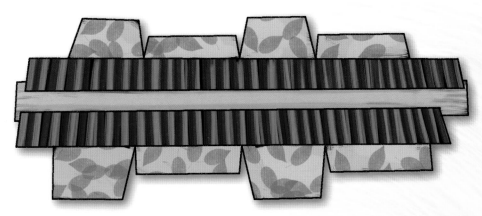

2. Cut strips of duct tape that are longer than your box. Lay a strip of color A across the middle. Then, slightly overlapping each strip, alternate color A and color B until the box is completely covered.

3. Trim the duct tape from the open areas between the outer flaps. Fold over the extra tape on the ends. Use a craft knife to cut out the hole for the tissues.

4. Refold the box along its original **creases** and place the tissues back inside. Seal the flaps closed with matching tape.

A USEFUL BOX
Once all of the tissues in your box are used up, you can place it on your desk and use it to store pens, pencils, and other small items. Or maybe you could use it to display your duct tape flowers!

Soft Stadium Seat

Woo-hoo! It's fun to cheer on a team from the sidelines. But sitting in bleachers for a whole game can get uncomfortable. Bring this stadium cushion to your next sporting event. Decorate it with your team's colors to show your support.

Materials
- Bubble wrap
- 2 colors/patterns of duct tape (color A and color B)
- Ruler
- Scissors

Steps

1. Fold or stack pieces of bubble wrap to make a square about 16 inches (40 cm) on each side and about 2 inches (5 cm) thick. Tape it together with some small pieces of duct tape.

2. Cut a strip of color A that is a little wider than the bubble wrap "pillow." Tape it across the center of the pillow.

3. Continue laying strips of color A above and below the middle strip, overlapping slightly, until the entire surface is covered.

4. Trim the edges even, and fold them over onto the edges of the cushion. (It's okay if the edges are a little rough. You'll be covering them with an edge piece.)

5. Flip the cushion over and repeat steps 2 to 4 on the second side.
6. Cut a strip of color B that is a little wider than the pillow. Lay it across the bottom edge, and then fold it over to close the opening. Repeat on the top. Trim the edges.
7. Cover the sides of the cushion with strips of color B. Trim the edges.
8. Make two handles with color B (*see page 11*) that are about 12 inches (30 cm) long.
9. Stick the handles along the top edge. Cover the base of each handle with color A.

LINE UP!
When you are using a duct tape with a pattern, try to line it up as best you can so no one will notice the seams between strips.

Cover It Up!

You can make colorful duct tape creations for all parts of your day. Start the morning using a toothbrush with a colorful handle. Cover a notebook or binder to use at school. Decorate a lunch box with stripes of patterned tape. Make a wallet to hold your allowance. Tape a fringed flower to the end of your pencil to make homework more fun. The ideas are endless!

You can cover your world with color. You can share the color, too. Duct tape creations make great gifts to spread your creativity around.

Glossary

adhesive (ad-HEE-siv) a substance, such as glue, that makes things stick together

alternate (AWL-tur-nayt) go back and forth between two things

ammunition (am-yuh-NISH-uhn) bullets or shells that can be fired from weapons

bond (BAHND) a force that holds objects together

creases (KREE-siz) folds or lines in fabric or paper

duct (DUHKT) a tube that carries air or liquid from one place to another

durable (DOOR-uh-buhl) tough and lasting for a long time

flexible (FLEK-suh-buhl) able to bend

precise (pri-SISE) very accurate or exact

reinforce (ree-in-FORS) to make something stronger or more secure

resourceful (ri-SORS-fuhl) able to solve problems in creative ways

technicians (tek-NISH-uhnz) people who work with specialized equipment or do practical laboratory work

For More Information

Books

Bell-Rehwoldt, Sheri. *The Kids' Guide to Duct Tape Projects*. Mankato, MN: Capstone Press, 2012.

Dobson, Jolie. *The Duct Tape Book*. Richmond Hill, Ontario, CAN: Firefly Books, 2012.

Morgan, Richela Fabian. *Tape It and Make It: 101 Duct Tape Activities.* Hauppauge, NY: Barron's, 2012.

Wallenfang, Patti. *Just Duct Tape It!* Little Rock, AR: Leisure Arts, 2011.

Web Sites

Duck® Brand—Ducktivities

http://duckbrand.com/duck-tape-club/ducktivities

Find and share ideas for making crafts, clothes, and other creations with duct tape.

Exploratorium

www.exploratorium.edu

This museum's Web site encourages curious thinkers and creators.

Index

About the Author

Dana Meachen Rau is the author of more than 300 books for children on many topics, including science, history, cooking, and crafts. She creates, experiments, researches, and writes from her home office in Burlington, Connecticut.